THE 5 STEP RELATIONSHIP BLUEPRINT

Other Books by Calvin Witcher

PARENTING WITH PIECES

150 DAYS OF PEACE

THE 5 STEP RELATIONSHIP BLUEPRINT

PEACE 101

TELL THEM

Other Co-Authored Books with Calvin Witcher

The Better Business Book

CalvinWitcher.com

THE 5 STEP RELATIONSHIP BLUEPRINT

HOW TO CREATE CONSCIOUS AND CONNECTED RELATIONSHIPS

CALVIN WITCHER

WITCHER
PUBLISHING GROUP

The 5 Step Relationship Blueprint. How To Create Conscious And Connected Relationships.
Copyright © 2017+ by Calvin Witcher.

Published and distributed by Witcher Publishing Group.

Cover Design: Calvin Witcher
Interior Design: Calvin Witcher

This book may be purchased in bulk for educational, business, fundraising, or sales promotional use. For Information, please email info@witcherpublishing.com

Publishing consultation, support, design, and composition by Witcher Publishing Group. **www.witcherpublishing.com**.

Library of Congress Cataloging-in-Publication Data

Trade Paperback ISBN: 978-0-9971151-6-1
E-book ISBN: 978-0-9971151-7-8

Witcher Publishing Group - rev. date: 02/26/2017

Witcher Publishing Group
Visit WitcherPublishing.com

Welcome & Hello My Friend,

Thank you for taking the time to view this relationship resource. I'm honored to partner with you in building a relationship that is dynamic in quality, designed with you in mind, and ultimately destined for your continual success.

I know that relationships have their celebrations and they also have their challenges. The first thing I'd like for you to know is that you're not alone.

Experiencing challenges in your relationship does not make you weak – it makes you a worker. Anyone that is continually working on themselves and their relationship will inevitably encounter some rough patches. This is normal.

If you're currently single, use this resource as a way of setting a foundation that will set you up for success in your future relationship.

There's one thing I want you to know before we begin! You have the power to change anything and everything about your life and I'm here to help you do just that!

I trust this book will serve as an investment in your life and relationship.

All the best!

Calvin Witcher

Table of Contents

So, What Are The 5 Steps?

DEFINE THE RELATIONSHIP
TALK ABOUT THE THEME
PRIORITIZE YOUR STRENGTHS
SCHEDULE YOUR SUCCESS
ALWAYS SEEK SUPPORT

Let's Dive In Now

Introduction

ᛜ

Oh, how we love to love!

What a wonderful feeling love is. It seems that from infancy through adulthood, we are all programmed to seek intimate relationships. And, if you don't have a relationship, then something is wrong with you.

We observe couples walking on the street, holding hands, laughing, and all without a care in the world. We watch television shows of happy and thriving families and, sprinkled periodically throughout the show, commercials are peddling passionate relationships. Then, when you are online you're bombarded with advertisements from companies encouraging you to get married. If that wasn't enough, you're then assaulted by strangers announcing their engagement.

The subtle suggestion is that people that are happy are in relationships.

It seems that everyone has someone...*Except you*.

Many of us have bought into this picturesque view of relationships and, consequently, are disappointed when our life doesn't reflect the image we've seen in the media.

I don't say this to discourage you but rather to help you understand that, we've all been led to believe that love and life only happens one way.

I want to let you know that life, and especially relationships, is not a one size fits all experience.

You get the opportunity to design and determine the life that's best for YOU!

But before you go deep into design mode, let's talk about what relationships are and what they aren't.

So, What Is A Relationship?

Relationships are a part of every aspect of our society and always will be. Relationships are professional, parental, situational, and yes – personal.

The dictionary defines a relationship[i] as:
- *a connection, association, or involvement or*
- *an emotional or other connection between people*

Whether it's romantic, professional, or otherwise, relationships are all about connection. So, really this conversation about having better relationships is about having better connections.

Part of this journey of life is about learning how to manage the relationships we already have and having stronger connective points within it.

Connections join two or more things together. This connection must be strong if you expect to weather the challenging times. Connections are like chain links. If there's a weak point in a chain link, then that is the first place that will break under pressure.

Connection Starts With You

If you want a strong connection point, you must start by being a strong connected person - FIRST. Did you get that?

The relationship that you will always have and can never escape is the one with yourself. Your personal connection with who you are must always remain strong. If you ever find that you're "disconnected" with parts of your life, this is usually a sore point in your relationship. You'll likely, and unconsciously, want your partner to resolve this or "compensate" for this need in your life.

So Yes, connection is essential.

This is vital to understand especially as you begin uniting with someone else in other relationship dynamics.

How you feel about you is important. I would even say that how you feel about you is foundational to a healthy relationship. Period. And, this goes both ways.

You must feel good about yourself, your values, and everything that is collectively YOU. And, your partner must do the same.

I've been a spiritual counselor, executive life coach and mentor for over 20 years and I constantly hear individuals say that they're looking for someone to "complete them". This is a dangerous way of thinking about yourself and your life.

50% from you and 50% from your spouse does not equal 100% in a relationship.

1/2 of you and 1/2 your spouse does not equal a whole relationship.

Oftentimes, when someone says the above statement, they are looking for someone to fill the voids in their own life, complete the incomplete, or strengthen their existing weaknesses.

We receive the energy we give. Relationships should be about complementing each other not completing each other. A relationship will only expose, expand, and exaggerate what exists.

In other words, this means that if you feel insecure now, then you'll likely attract another insecure person and/or your insecurity will increase when in a relationship.

So forth, and so on...

Now, if relationships are all about connection and complementing us and not about completing us, then why do we seek them so much?

Why Do We Seek Relationships?

Life is full of many changes. I believe that one of the ways we find stability, safety, and security in our lives is by having a "constant". A constant is routine and expected in our lives. It's something we don't have to think about because it's always there. That constant is the one thing in our lives that remains still, steady, and solid in the face of an ever-changing world.

Oftentimes, relationships provide that constant that we seek. This is also why we put so much emphasis on long term relationships.

Relationships can go to the core of who we are. Therefore, we will do anything and everything possible to fight for our relationship.

When our foundation and stability is threatened, this is when our relationships tend to fall on hard times and sometimes fall apart.

When Times Get Hard

Every relationship goes through rough times. I know this isn't always a comfortable situation but you should know that it happens to everyone.

This resource is designed to help you **repair** your relationship, **refocus** your energy, **restructure** your life, **recommit** to yourself, and **reconnect** with your partner.

This work of building relationships is all designed, and like every good design, it needs a blueprint.

This is yours!

The 5 Step Relationship Blueprint details how to:
1. Define The Relationship
2. Talk About The Theme
3. Prioritize Your Strengths
4. Schedule Your Success
5. Always Seek Support

Let's Begin.

Define The Relationship

❧

While these steps are not necessarily in sequential order, I do put great emphasis on this first point. You must **Define The Relationship**. Now, what do I mean by this? Let me explain it like this.

Many people embark upon a relationship not having clear boundaries and without a clear picture of why they fell in love with their spouse.

This can be a problem. This can lead to unmet expectations. And, if not resolved, this will eventually grow into resentment because it can make you feel like your partner has changed or you're not getting your needs met.

All of this could have been avoided and can be avoided by taking the time to define the relationship.

Defining the relationship simply means to *clearly understand the role that you and your partner have in the relationship*. You must identify why you started a relationship with your spouse and vice versa. This must not be general.

It must be specific.

Defining the relationship is really about clarity of roles and how each person shows up and shines through the relationship.

Everyone has a part that they play in a relationship, however, many don't know what that role is. Remember that earlier we discussed that relationships are about complementing each other.

It's difficult (and nearly impossible) to complement something or someone that is undefined.

You must define everything!

Now, I know what you may be thinking. "Calvin, this sounds unromantic and like you're boxing my relationship in a corner." Well, to an extent, I am. I am trying to corner you, but only to help you positively grow your relationship.

I believe that the more we know about ourselves and our spouse, the more we can greater serve the relationship.

Frederick Douglass once said, "Knowledge makes a man (or woman) unfit to be a slave."[ii] WOW! This is such a powerful statement.

Could it be that you're feeling trapped, or a "slave" to your relationship, because you don't have the knowledge you need? Maybe you feel enslaved because you don't know what will make your partner happy, or make you happy. Maybe you feel stuck because you don't have the tools necessary to get you out of the repetitive cycle of frustration and fighting.

Knowledge is not just power – It is a portal to everything you want. You hold the power to change your life and your relationship for the better.

One of the easiest and fastest ways to help you define your relationship is by asking yourself the following questions:

- **"What did I expect my partner to do when we got together?"**

- **"Who did I think my partner was when we first met?"**

- **"Did I know who I was when my partner and I first met?"**

- **"Did I know what I wanted in a relationship when we got together?"**

These are powerful questions that can help you on this journey.

Here's a good example that I often find with business owners. If you're an entrepreneur, did you expect your spouse to help you in the business and partner with you in this venture? Does your spouse not meet this expectation? Are you constantly fighting with your spouse to help you in your business? Do you not feel supported? Could it be that you didn't fully define the relationship in the beginning?

In this scenario, maybe you put your spouse in this position to fill a void in your company, but it wasn't their passion or purpose and now it's causing nothing but problems. Let's solve this and define the relationship. Maybe your partner is meant to be your cheerleader rather than your co-worker.

This simple refocusing can save you many fights and much frustration. Take this example and look at your own relationship structure to determine how you can better define your relationship.

As you fine tune your definition of your relationship, I encourage you to **Talk About The Theme**.

Talk About The Theme

℘

Now, this one is fun for me. Our next focus in **The 5 Step Relationship Blueprint** is, "**Talk About The Theme**".

Every relationship has a theme. Every family has a focus. Let me give you a couple of examples that will support this idea.

If I say, "Trump", who and what do you think about?

That's right! You probably thought of Donald Trump and Real Estate – almost immediately. The 'Trump' name and brand is synonymous with Real Estate. The Trump family may have several business ventures, many hobbies and a diverse set of likes and dislikes but, in the end, they are known collectively for one thing – Real Estate.

No matter how you feel about the Trump family there is one undeniable fact. Their theme is Real Estate.

Let's try one more time.

If I say, "Jackson", who and what do you think about?

You probably thought about "The Jacksons" and specifically Janet and Michael Jackson. You may have thought about "The Jackson 5". When someone says, "The Jacksons", it usually is about music.

So, the "theme" of the Jacksons is clearly Music!

Now, I'm sure that the Trump's, Jackson's, Bush's, and many other well-known families didn't consciously sit down and say, "Hey, family our theme is _____". I would suspect that this theme came out of a common interest and a common intent.

That's exactly what I'm talking about regarding your relationship. You need to know your common interests and common intents.

I encourage you to think about your relationship as a brand. What would be the unique quality of your family?

How would you describe your relationship and family distinction?

A good way of determining what your relationship theme is rests in asking several key questions.

- **What are we known for as a couple/family?**
- **What do I want us to be known for?**
- **When someone thinks of our relationship or family, what do they think?**

Every relationship and family has a theme – including yours! You just need to begin to answer the questions above.

When you acknowledge the theme of your relationship, it often requires you to **Prioritize Your Strengths**.

Prioritize Your Strengths

ଔ

Everyone has a 'need', and everyone has a 'strength'. I'm sure you noticed that I'm using the word 'need' rather than 'weakness'. This is because when we think of a 'weakness', we often think of something that we can't change or is a defect. Having a 'need' denotes that we can do something about it. We can fulfill needs in our life and, when we do, we feel confident and empowered.

We all have needs. And, we all have strengths.

Many times, in our relationships, we focus so much attention on the things we're not doing right. We concern ourselves with all the things that need to change in the relationship.

In the many years that I've been counseling couples, I've discovered couples are just too hard on themselves.

We put too much pressure on things that are not core values. And simply put, the things we complain about today, will likely not be a concern in the future.

Sometimes, you need to just **let it go** and **go with the flow**. Now, that's not to say that you don't take responsibility for things that can help improve your relationship. I'm not saying that at all. What I am saying is that everything is not a priority at the same time.

I encourage you to prioritize the strengths in your relationships rather than focusing on the things that need to change.

So, what are your strengths? And, what do you bring to the table?

We all have something that we're good at doing! Your partner has strengths also. Even if you're in a rough patch with your partner, you can find at least one thing about them that they do uniquely well.

Try it right now.

I want you to get a piece of paper and write down all the strengths of your partner.

Here's an example. Maybe your partner is good at washing the laundry but not ironing the clothes? Skip the things that are a need for them...in this case ironing the clothes. Just write down, "My partner is really good at <u>washing the laundry</u>."

Make a game out of it and see how many things you can list!

You'd be surprised how many times we overlook the good things in our spouse because we're so concerned with the things that need improving.

Prioritize Your Strengths by bringing the good things of your relationship back into focus. Then, let everything else go.

When you have the good things in line, you can then enhance your relationship and **Schedule Your Success**.

Schedule Your Support

☙

Relationships that have strong connections are steady and consistent. Consistency is a trait that you can learn to use if you want to have strong relationships.

Scheduling Your Success is all about creating a plan, writing it down, implementing the plan, and adjusting as needed.

Good and healthy relationships are no accident. It takes work and planning.

If I looked at your calendar right now, how many date nights would I see? How much personal time would I see?

Do you have a time to discuss finances? When do you shop for groceries or complete other errands?

This may seem like an unnecessary task, but it's not. Our lives are full of so many obligations and responsibilities. If not careful, our relationships can feel like "one more chore" that we need to do among the sea of many other chores.

You need to have time by yourself. I'm sure you love your spouse but you also need a break from them as well. Go ahead and schedule that in. When you schedule time just for yourself, this gives you moments that you can just break away and have a life outside of who you are in the relationship.

This is necessary.

You also need to have dedicated times with your spouse. This time should be uninterrupted.

Research shows that we are more likely to keep an appointment if it is recorded somewhere. Of course, I always suggest using an electronic calendar or scheduling app but if you prefer the traditional calendar – just do it.

Schedules can be a tricky endeavor because life happens and changes do need to be made. Try not to create a habit of changing things that are on the calendar.

Remember, you are going for consistency here which means we need to create a pattern that supports that effort.

I use calendars often with my clients because it helps me track the progress they have made and remind them of the milestones they have achieved. It's also good for helping them remain accountable for the things they agreed to work on.

As you're scheduling your success, you may find you need to seek support. If so, reach out and don't be afraid to ask for help.

Always Seek Support

◌

To me, this is one of those no brainer situations, so I'll keep it simple. **Always Seek Support**. Period. This may sound simple to do but it's often the one step that gets overlooked the most.

I can understand why couples don't seek support during challenging times. It takes courage and humility to admit you need help. I get that. I think it's common sense to ask for help when you need it and I also understand the pain associated with admitting that you don't have all the answers.

Common sense is not always common practice, right? We must practice how to ask for help and we also should practice humility when receiving that help.

If you need support to help get your relationship out of a challenge or crisis, then don't hesitate to contact our office as soon as possible.

There's always an answer, but you must act.

Conclusion

⌀

Since you're reading this, I know that you deeply care about having meaningful, conscious, and connected relationships!

Thank you so much for sharing your time with me and beginning the process for a healthier life and relationship.

You may have noticed that I didn't really talk about the love aspect in relationships and that's for a reason. I'm a firm believer that relationships don't have emotion problems, they have efficiency problems.

I often find that love is never the problem. Committing to do things that support love is usually at the heart of everything.

I designed this resource to focus on that one objective.

I trust that this information has helped expand how you view your relationships.

I hope that you received some new insights that you can implement in your personal life as well.

As a reminder, I'm here to help support you personally and in your relationship.

Feel free to reach out and I'd love to partner with you! You can contact me through my website **CalvinWitcher.com**.

About The Author

୶

CALVIN WITCHER is an Author, Teacher and Spiritual Crusader that has coached international teachers, doctors, therapists, business professionals and individuals seeking clarity. Known for his bold and integrative approach to spirituality, he calls all to freedom and the soul's highest calling.

Calvin is the host of his self-help show on YouTube, and his podcast, Expect Great Things, which debuted in the Top 30 Spirituality Video Podcasts on iTunes. He is a sought after thought-leader, conference speaker, and workshop facilitator in the fields of philosophy, spirituality, and personal development and has been featured in Success Magazine.

As a gifted counselor and speaker, the core of Calvin's message is "helping others find clarity through challenge, crisis, and change". Transcending socioeconomic and denominational barriers, his message resonates among people from every walk of life.

With a faith, undaunted by the task at hand, this husband, father, and mentor is the prophetic voice to a progressive generation. Today, as a much-in-demand speaker and proclaimer of inclusivity and interfaith, he continues to fulfill his mission to radically heal and transform lives.

Calvin Witcher is available for speaking, teaching, consulting and counseling. For media inquiries, ideas for collaboration and more information, **Please Visit CalvinWitcher.com**

More Products And Offerings From Calvin

⊗

Books

150 DAYS OF PEACE
– Devotional & Journal –

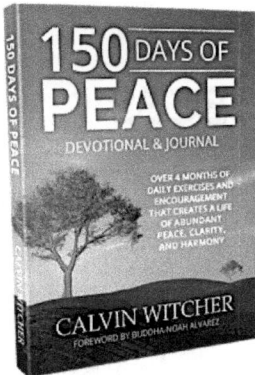

Over 4 Months Of Daily Exercises And Encouragement That Creates A Life Of Abundant Peace, Clarity, And Harmony

How do we form new habits? The simple answer is practice. Many of us desire to get rid of negative habits and create new positive habits. Whatever we desire to see in our life, we must put the structure in place to support our needs and wants.

150 Days of Peace – Devotional & Journal is a step-by-step process for creating more peace, clarity, and harmony throughout your day.

This daily devotional and journal is designed to guide you into a thriving and transformed life.

With loads of quotes and commentary, this book is the starting point for a successful day. We all desire a roadmap that leads us from our present problems to a place of power and peace. This book maps out the way.

ENJOY THE JOURNEY AS IT CONTINUALLY UNFOLDS.

Get Your Copy At CalvinWitcher.com or Wherever Books Are Sold

PARENTING WITH PIECES

Parenting As A Catalyst For Personal Growth

Discover what progress REALLY looks like when you get YOUR needs met first!

Introducing Parenting with Pieces — a groundbreaking book that will accelerate your personal growth and radically improve your effectiveness as a parent — piece by piece.

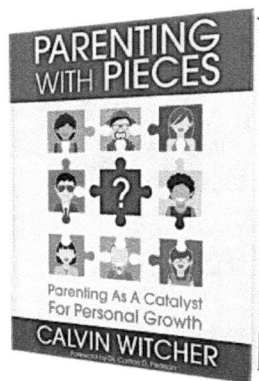

Here's a sample of what you will learn from this book:

- How to eliminate thoughts that question your ability to be a "good parent"
- How to balance your personal needs with the demands of building a family
- How to use proven psychological tools to help resolve your internal conflicts
- How to break negative cycles that come from your childhood experiences
- How to achieve personal happiness by identifying patterns that exaggerate unnecessary stress in your life
- How to overcome self-criticism by redefining who you are as a parent
  and much more...

Get Your Copy At CalvinWitcher.com or Wherever Books Are Sold

Work With Calvin

COACHING & MENTORING

Are you ready to embrace all that you were meant to be?

Calvin Witcher offers 1-on-1 sessions through holistic life coaching and spiritual mentoring. He will help you find clarity through every challenge, crisis and change of your life.

Are you searching for personal growth, professional development, or leadership training? Do you understand that there is more to your life than what you have been experiencing? Yes, you do! And, this is what you have been looking for! Your life will change for the better, and so too will the lives of those you impact.

Calvin Invites You To Experience Your Own Private Coaching Sessions.

Look at some of our 5-Star Yelp reviews![iii]

Alexander N.
Claremont, CA
3 friends
9 reviews

⭐⭐⭐⭐⭐ 7/8/2016

First to Review

Calvin exudes more positive energy than anyone I have ever met. His positive energy, his wisdom and his caring for creating positive change in others make him an extraordinary person. I am fortunate for the opportunity to know Calvin and to listen and apply his wisdom to my life.

Thank you Calvin for injecting your energy into our community. Keep up the great work!

Jack P.
Oakland, CA
0 friends
2 reviews

⭐⭐⭐⭐⭐ 10/10/2016

Calvin is an INCREDIBLE counselor and coach. He helped me go from overwhelm to deep, centered confidence and inner power. I'm so grateful for the work that we did together!

Are One-On-One Sessions For You?

- One-On-One Sessions Are For Individuals Incorporating Calvin's Principles Effectively, And Those Who Want To Keep Developing Their Experience To Fully Achieve Their Unique Destiny.

- One-On-One Sessions Are For Those Who Are Curious About An In-Depth Revelation Of Their Spiritual Awareness Their True God Nature.

- One-On-One Sessions Are For People Who Want To Create A Life That Reflects Their Core Beliefs But Are Aware Of A Gap Between How They

Want Things To Be And How They Currently Experiencing Their Reality.

- One-On-One Sessions Are For People That Have The Courage To Grow Despite Adversity, Change Even When It's Uncomfortable, And For People That Are Seeking To Live In Their Genius.

Audrey C.
Los Angeles, CA
1 friend
6 reviews

⭐⭐⭐⭐⭐ 8/1/2016

Calvin is extremely approachable, has a very positive attitude and a very unique approach to counseling and providing comfort to his clients. I consulted him on a few aspects on my relationship experiences and the suggestions he provided were very original and something I've never thought of to practice to achieve manifestation. His spiritual guidance and intuition guided me through a difficult time and I will definitely revisit again! Thank you Calvin:)!

Noah A.
Los Angeles, CA
4 friends
11 reviews

⭐⭐⭐⭐⭐ 7/9/2016

Clear-thinking, clear-seeing, and direct in action. These are the valuable, bold skills that Calvin utilizes in his guidance and every day connection. Not only does Calvin offer pointed energetic wisdom and spirit-centered solutions, but his words land high and have a unique way of nestling into the practical-positive, which lends toward genuine elevation in life, consciousness, and one's daily walk. I highly recommend Mr. Witcher for life coaching, intuitive business counsel, and spiritual development!

To submit your information to Calvin for coaching and mentoring, please visit **CalvinWitcher.com**

Notes

[i] relationship. (n.d.). Dictionary.com Unabridged. Retrieved February 27, 2017 from Dictionary.com website
http://www.dictionary.com/browse/relationship
[ii] Goodreads - Goodreads Inc. -
http://www.goodreads.com/author/quotes/18943.Frederick_Douglass
[iii] Calvin Witcher Reviews. Yelp.com –
https://www.yelp.com/biz/calvin-witcher-dallas